W9-BXP-764

© 2021 Connor Boyack
All rights reserved.

No graphic, visual, electronic, film, microfilm, tape recording, or any other means may be used to reproduce in any form, without prior written permission of the author, except in the case of brief passages embodied in critical reviews and articles.

ISBN 978-1-943521-65-4

Boyack, Connor, author.
Stanfield, Elijah, illustrator.
The Tuttle Twins and the Leviathan Crisis / Connor Boyack.

Cover design by Elijah Stanfield
Edited and typeset by Connor Boyack

Printed in the United States

THE TUTTLE TWINS
and the
LEVIATHAN CRISIS

To all truth tellers in tough times.

If ever a team of heroes was
needed, it's you, and now.

It was a fairly quiet Saturday morning at the Main Street Plaza, with few cars in the parking lot or customers shopping in the businesses.

At Infinite Adventures Comics and Games, however, things were very busy—a fact you could tell from the overflowing bike rack. The store was hosting an event for a new adventure game called Team of Heroes that had become really popular.

In the playing area, there was an energetic feeling in the air. It was full of kids, teens, and a few adults, too. This new game seemed to be enjoyed by people of all ages.

Part of the reason that the game had caught on so quickly was a built-in incentive to play often. As players completed quests, their heroes got Level Up tokens, which they could exchange for Power Boost cards for their characters.

Ethan and Emily Tuttle bought a starter deck of cards and selected their hero characters. A few of their friends—Tashi, Aaron, and Brooklyn—had joined them so they could form a team.

"Welcome, everyone," Mike, the store manager, announced. "I will be your story master for today's quest. It's a really exciting one that I came up with. Who's ready?"

Everyone cheered as Mike pulled out a binder labeled *The Leviathan Crisis* to begin the story.

"What's in there?" asked Brooklyn.

"You'll find out soon enough," Mike said, "but I must warn you that *this* quest isn't just about battles and magic—it's about strategy, teamwork, and imagination." He paused and grinned. "So, Team of Heroes, get ready to have some fun!"

For nearly two hours, they explored their new world. Ethan's cards gave his large Ogre character a golden gauntlet and an axe. "Arrgh, smash!" Ethan said whenever he rolled dice.

Emily's character was a paladin warrior named Libertas. She had a sword of truth and a shield of virtue. Their teammates' characters included a great archer, an elemental warlock, and an inventor with a space-age suit. Their combined powers seemed to make them a great team.

"Here are your Level Up tokens," Mike told their team as they completed one of their challenges. "And it's good timing, because a new crisis looms in our midst."

The kids bought some Power Boost packs and began showing off their new weapons, charms, and skills. To Emily's surprise, hers included an embossed foil card—the Idol of Leviathan!

"That sounds like a really powerful card!" Aaron said. "And our quest is called The Leviathan Crisis, so it'll probably be perfect to use."

"Speaking of a crisis..." Mike interrupted, placing a small statue on the table. "DemiGog, Queen of Crisis, has summoned her hordes to the Village of the Vale! To arms, Heroes!"

The team began exchanging blows with the hordes and building up defenses to protect the village.

"Uh oh, I rolled a twelve!" Mike said. "DemiGog now uses her Clouded Mind spell, which confuses the villagers to attack the Heroes." The twins and their friends were quickly learning what a powerful enemy the DemiGog was.

"Prepare for defeat," Mike told the team as they began to panic.

"Wait, so how do we fight off the villagers, too?" Tashi wondered. The kids were worried they would lose because they didn't fully understand the many parts of the game yet.

"I'll use the Idol of Leviathan!" Emily announced. "The instructions say that if we surrender our Power Boosts to the Idol then it will combine our weapons, charms, and skills to stop any crisis. But it also says the team has to vote to use it."

"Do it!" the team shouted unanimously.

Emily rolled a ten, which was good enough for the Idol of Leviathan to stop DemiGog's Clouded Mind spell and drive away the horde. The team erupted with cheers of relief. They were saved!

"We won! Does that mean we get more Level Up tokens?" Emily asked.

"Actually, the unique effect of using that card is that the Idol levels up," Mike replied. "It becomes more powerful—not you."

Ethan suddenly had a thought: "So if our team now has a way stop any crisis, why wouldn't we want to use it all the time?"

"Never let a good crisis go to waste, right?" Mike said, giving Emily the little DemiGog statue. "How about you hold on to this until next week's quest."

The twins sped off toward home, passing a nearby shop owner putting up a sign on one of his windows. They didn't think much of it until they noticed another business with a similar sign nearby.

"Hey, Dad!" Emily shouted, riding up onto the driveway. He had still been asleep when they had left earlier that morning.

Mr. Tuttle had been working very late hours and hadn't been home as much. The twins noticed he was getting ready to leave yet again.

"You have to work on a Saturday?" Ethan groaned.

"We have an emergency meeting," Mr. Tuttle replied. "We may have to lay off some of our employees so the company doesn't run out of money."

Ethan wondered if the trouble with his dad's company was related to the troubles of the other businesses around town. "Is something happening with the economy?" he asked.

"Big time," Mr. Tuttle said somberly. "Say, want to come with me? I can try to explain in the car."

The trio hopped in the truck and began the drive to the office.

"There are a lot of chaotic things happening lately," said Mr. Tuttle as he drove. "And people are afraid and can't guess what will happen next. So, instead of taking risks to invest in new opportunities, they hold onto their money until the future is clearer."

"Imagine exploring uncharted land," he added. "On a clear day you can see what direction you should go—but if the air was misty, it wouldn't be wise to move forward without knowing what's ahead."

CLEAR FUTURE

"So if people are holding on to their money, then that must mean businesses aren't earning much right now," Emily observed.

"And that probably means businesses stop producing as much new stuff," Ethan added.

"Right, and that's called a *recession*," Mr. Tuttle said. "But it can also be helpful, giving people time to figure out the right path forward with their money."

UNCLEAR FUTURE

An advertisement began playing on the radio for Bernadine Cortez, a candidate trying to become the country's president.

"During scary times such as these, it's important that we elect leaders with a master plan," Cortez said. "I will get the economy going again by giving everyone stimulus money. No one will have to live in fear of losing their job. A vote for me is a..."

Mr. Tuttle quickly turned off the radio, letting out a sound of disgust. "These politicians are so full of promises," he said. "But they're nothing more than demagogues."

The twins exchanged surprised glances. "Wait, did you say DemiGog?" Emily asked.

"A *demagogue* is a person who tries to get power by *exploiting* people's emotions—in other words, taking advantage of their fear," Mr. Tuttle explained. "Lots of people are losing their jobs right now, and they are scared. So politicians are using this crisis as an opportunity to get more power."

"Never let a good crisis go to waste..." Ethan said softly, recalling what Mike said after their game. "Interesting."

Emily looked at her DemiGog statue, wondering why it had that name.

"But if stimulus money could help people keep their jobs, why wouldn't we want that?" Ethan asked. "Couldn't that help your business right now?"

"Would you take medicine if it was worse than the disease?" Mr. Tuttle replied. "There will always be crises—natural disasters, viruses, recessions... but people need to be free to make their own choices. Instead, demagogues want to take those choices away; they want to be in charge and control us.

"They'll just march us into the mist without knowing the best way," he continued. "And it always leads to even more problems. Demagogues have done this throughout history, but people are *ignorant* of this pattern, so it happens again and again."

"That sounds like what Grandma Tuttle says," Emily replied. "Those who don't learn from the past are..."

"...condemned to repeat it," Ethan finished for her.

"The promises these politicians make are like a Trojan horse," Mr. Tuttle said. "Ever heard of that?"

"I actually just watched a video about it," Ethan said, explaining to Emily. "It's how the Greeks won the Trojan War—they built a big wooden horse, hid some men inside, then pretended to sail away."

"The Trojans pulled the horse into their city as a trophy, but when it was nighttime, the men inside snuck out, unlocked the city gates, and let the returning Greek army in to crush the Trojans."

"That's how the myth goes," Mr. Tuttle said. "So, a *Trojan horse* is when someone tries to deceive us into thinking something is helpful or good when, in reality, it will harm us."

They arrived at Mr. Tuttle's office. Ethan noticed an empty building across the parking lot where there used to be a restaurant just weeks before.

"Hi, Mary!" the twins said in unison as Mr. Tuttle left them at the front desk to head into the conference room. Mary grabbed them some cream-filled pastries from the break room.

Ethan took a newspaper from the desk. "People still read these things?" he teased, flipping the pages.

There were stories about businesses failing, the economy, and protests by people wanting the government to do more to help. On another page, a bank owner wrote a letter, pleading with people to have more faith in the government's stimulus plans.

"Our society is growing weak," Mary said as she looked over Ethan's shoulder.

"What do you mean?" Emily asked.

"Well, people used to value personal responsibility," she replied. "But now when there are problems, people cry out for someone to save them—even to make choices for them. They act like children... no offense," she winked at the twins.

"Like this lady," Ethan said, pointing to a photo of Bernadine Cortez in the paper.

"Politicians like her love to say they can solve all our problems," Mary said. "That's why I think she likes how scared people are, so they ask her for help."

"It's *fearmongering*—encouraging people to be afraid. It's no wonder why Leviathan is so big."

"Leviathan?!" the twins said to one another. "It's like our game is suddenly real life!" exclaimed Ethan.

"*Leviathan* is a mythical monster that grew to be very large," Mary explained. "So it's a nickname to describe the ever-growing power of government."

She could tell that the twins were interested, so she continued.

"About a century ago, there was an economic recession, kind of like we have now," Mary said. "The people wanted the president, Herbert Hoover, to take control of the economy and make the recession stop."

"But Hoover warned them, 'Every collectivist revolution rides in on a Trojan horse of emergency.'"

"We know what that means," Ethan said. "During an emergency, our freedom can be taken in sneaky ways—like the Trojan horse!"

"Right. But against his better judgment," Mary said, "Hoover controlled the economy and the recession became so bad that they called it a depression."

"So he stopped, right?" Emily asked.

Mary chuckled a bit. "No, dear... Just like Leviathan, government never really shrinks—it's like a *ratchet effect* where things only go in one direction."

"In fact, most people were mad that Hoover didn't do more! So they elected the demagogue Franklin D. Roosevelt who pushed for a 'New Deal' to put the government in control even more. They told farmers how much to grow, how much things should cost, **and how** much people could be paid... **they even banned people from owning gold!**"

"These chaotic policies scared people from doing business, dragging out the depression many years... until another crisis came: World War II."

"We learned about Nazi Germany from our trip," Ethan said. "That war was definitely an awful crisis!"

"Leviathan grows the fastest in war," Mary said with a tone of disgust. "Politicians get excited when people are scared. They'll never let a crisis..."

"...go to waste." Emily finished.

"There are so many examples," Mary said. "After a terrorist attack, government claimed the power to spy through everyone's electronic devices! When people struggled to afford health care, the government tried to control it all and force people to buy health care plans they didn't want. And when there was a virus, government decided which businesses could stay open and whether we could meet with friends—we couldn't even sing at church without permission..."

"Leviathan is bigger than it's ever been," she sighed.

"But... if Leviathan never shrinks, that means it will eventually control everything," Ethan said hopelessly.

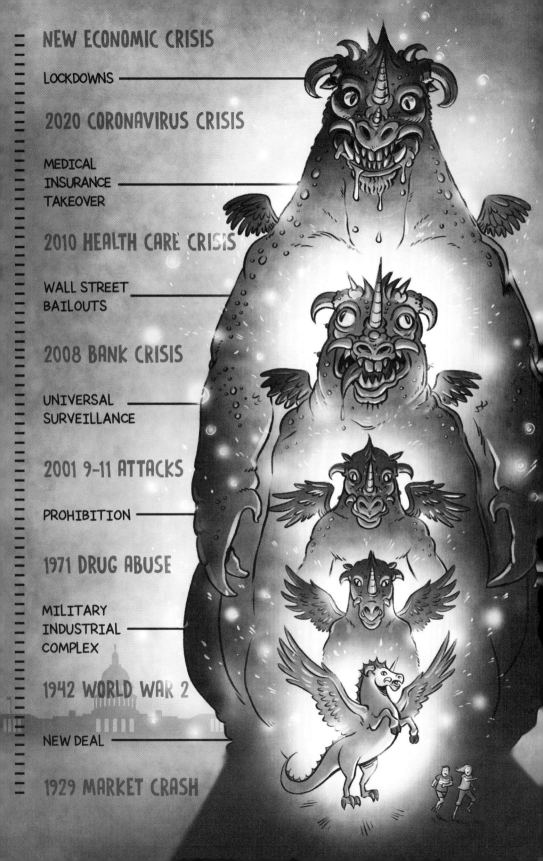

NEW ECONOMIC CRISIS

LOCKDOWNS ─────────

2020 CORONAVIRUS CRISIS

MEDICAL
INSURANCE ─────────
TAKEOVER

2010 HEALTH CARE CRISIS

WALL STREET ─────────
BAILOUTS

2008 BANK CRISIS

UNIVERSAL ─────────
SURVEILLANCE

2001 9-11 ATTACKS

PROHIBITION ─────────

1971 DRUG ABUSE

MILITARY
INDUSTRIAL ─────────
COMPLEX

1942 WORLD WAR 2

NEW DEAL ─────────

1929 MARKET CRASH

"How are we not essential?!" a voice erupted from the conference room. It was Tom, Mr. Tuttle's business partner, who was clearly upset. Ethan and Emily could easily overhear the conversation. Tom wanted to get the *stimulus*—"free money" from the government—but the government website said their company wasn't "essential" and didn't qualify.

"It's for the best," Mr. Tuttle told Tom as they exited room. "Frankly, I'm more worried about saving our freedoms than saving the company. When we're all scared like this, that's exactly when the government tries to control us even more."

INDIVIDUAL CHOICE

"I've always admired your strong beliefs," Tom said, "but I think electing Cortez is our best shot at getting the economy moving. We could use the stimulus checks, and so could our employees."

"It's not anyone else's responsibility to save jobs, or our company," Mr. Tuttle replied. "I have confidence in our ability to make the right choices for our business. Cortez doesn't know what's best for us!"

"Then, I'll let *you* be the one to tell Rebecca that she no longer has a job," Tom huffed as he headed for the office door.

GOVERNMENT
CONTROL

Mr. Tuttle saw the newspaper with the photo of Cortez and promptly threw it in the trash.

"Will the business be alright?" Emily asked.

"It should be," Mr. Tuttle sighed. "I need to call Rebecca."

He walked back into the conference room to make the call. Rebecca was a newer employee who the twins really liked. They listened as Mr. Tuttle explained he had to end her employment, and that she should come in on Monday to collect her things and get her final paycheck.

"It's too bad that government stimulus couldn't help us and save my job," she replied, tearing up.

"Rebecca, you're a very talented, hard-working person," Mr. Tuttle said. "Things are dark now, but it will be light again. There are other opportunities that will come along. Please believe me."

The mood was somber as the Tuttle family drove home that evening. Mr. Tuttle was lost in thought, trying to figure out what he should do.

Ethan was gazing out the window as Emily flipped through her card deck to distract herself. She noticed her Sword of Truth card, and began to wonder how her Libertas character could use it to fight back against Leviathan's power.

The day's conversations swirled in her head as she began to realize how important the truth was to fight back against demagogues seeking power—the truth of history, the truth of what's inside deceptive Trojan horses, and the truth of how freedoms that are lost to Leviathan can't easily be gotten back.

"Penny for your thoughts," Ethan told her.

"I don't trust that Idol... and I think we've been going about these quests all wrong," she replied with a sly smile.

Other businesses may be struggling, but Infinite Adventures was swarming with customers.

"Who could have known comic books and card games would be in high demand during a crisis?" Ethan said as the twins found their teammates.

"Customers like you are all the stimulus my store needs!" Mike beamed with pride. "Everyone, get ready for today's quest!"

It had been a week since Emily's epiphany on the drive home. The twins had a new strategy to win.

The Tuttle twins' Team of Heroes understood the game much better this time. They were more creative and confident in their play—and used one another's strengths and powers to complete each quest and solve different challenges.

The twins hoped that because of this confidence, they would be able to convince their friends that they didn't have to rely on the Idol when the Queen of Crisis eventually returned—that they instead could win relying on their own power and plans.

"DemiGog brings earthquakes, fires, and floods!" Mike announced as he rolled the dice.

"Ah! We need to use the Idol of Leviathan!" Aaron said in a panic. "It's our only chance!"

"Hang on," Emily calmly replied. "We can solve this crisis like the other challenges. Tashi's card has power over the elements, and we can help him. Then we can level up instead of the Idol."

"We think the Idol is a Trojan horse—it's a trap," Ethan added. "We shouldn't vote to use it."

The twins' reasoning did not convince the others. They were too afraid of defeat. Ethan and Emily lost the vote, and the Idol was used.

"DemiGog loses," Mike observed. "Idol levels up."

This pattern continued for the next hour. At the end of each level, the DemiGog would send the team into a panic. No matter how much Ethan and Emily tried to convince their friends, they would always vote to use the Idol of Leviathan to try and win.

"Welcome to the final level, adventurers," Mike told the kids as he began playing some epic music to set the mood.

"What will the crisis be this time?" Brooklyn asked nervously. The kids were on the edges of their seats, waiting in anticipation.

"From the lava pits in the sea of monsters rises Leviathan!" Mike read from his binder, placing an oversized statue of the scariest monster the kids had ever seen on the table.

"How powerful is Leviathan?!" Tashi worriedly asked.

"Precisely as powerful as you all have made it through its Idol: master level 40," Mike answered. "DemiGog commands all to bow to Leviathan!"

"I told you!" Emily exclaimed in frustration. "We're still only at level eight!"

"Well, one thing is for sure," Ethan said, standing up on his chair. "Heroes never bow to Leviathan!"

Ethan brought the team into a huddle. "Listen, we are in this spot because we didn't understand some of the game's rules, but it's more than that. We have to understand our enemies."

"We gave them power because of our fear and ignorance. But I think there's still a way out..." Emily said, showing them her card combination.

"I think that might actually work!" Aaron whispered. "Especially if we use all of our characters' defense cards to protect you."

A confident smile broke out across Emily's face as she played her cards. Libertas' Sword of Truth was now amplified with the Beacon of Light and guarded by her teammates.

Mike described the outcome: rays of flaming white light shooting from Libertas' sword, extinguishing DemiGog's power and blinding Leviathan, who disappeared as if it were only a hallucination.

Their creative strategy had worked! And the team was no longer afraid. They had confidence in their own power and abilities.

The twins told their parents everything that happened that night over dinner.

"You learned how to stop a pretend Leviathan," Mrs. Tuttle said. "I only wish it were that easy in real life!"

"It wasn't easy, since everyone was afraid and wanted something to help them," Ethan said. "It was like they were under Clouded Mind spells and falling for Trojan horses. They helped their own enemy!"

That's why the truth is so powerful," Emily said, thinking of her Libertas character. "If people know history, they won't be as likely to grow government just because they want it to solve their problems."

The Tuttle family brainstormed reasons why the truth is not more well known. Later that night, the twins decided they would write a letter to the newspaper to teach others in the community about the truths they had learned.

"This same newspaper recently printed a letter from a banker saying we need more faith in politicians to solve our economic problems. But he's wrong."

It was a bold way to begin their letter, but the twins were determined to fight ignorance and fear.

"Politicians like problems because they can claim to have solutions," the twins continued. "But their solutions often create even more problems."

Mrs. Tuttle was an excellent editor and helped the twins clarify each sentence to be more impactful.

The twins searched through several books to find good examples from history to share in their article, to explain why people need to have faith in themselves and one another—not a big Leviathan government.

Over the next few days, Mr. Tuttle received dozens of messages at work asking if the children who wrote the article were his.

The City Herald

PROTEST

Multiple fires were reported across the city late Monday night. Stephan Haynes, a reporter for CCN, reported that downtown Kenosha is filled with smoke.

A car dealership that was seen up in flames during the first night of Kenosh's mostly peaceful protest,

The unrest continued overnight, as video appeared to show a second car dealership being looted, while others stomped on cars and pulled down street lights. Earlier, a furniture store was looted and set on fire. The Wisconsin Department of Corrections building was also reportedly set on fire.

Several businesses in the city's Uptown district were ablaze by 1 a.m., which one New York Times reporter called "Just a horrible scene." In one scene shared by a

Ethan and Emily were back at their dad's office a few weeks after the Team of Heroes defeated Leviathan and their letter was published.

The twins' letter had generated so much interest that it gave Mr. Tuttle the idea to create a company newsletter to inform their clients about what was happening in the economy so they could make better decisions for themselves and be less afraid.

Ethan and Emily helped think up topics to write about, but the most important contribution came from Emily, who suggested the newsletter's name: The Sword of Truth.

Tom motioned everyone over to his computer. "Hey, check this out!" he said. Over 500 people had already become paid subscribers, and some of them purchased additional things, helping their business succeed even more.

"Turns out you don't need the promises of a politician or a stimulus from Leviathan when you have the truth on your side," Mr. Tuttle winked.

"Well, the real truth is that there *is* no Leviathan—at least, there's no gigantic monster," Mary said. "The government is just people like us, some of whom want to control others and control the economy."

"I suppose it's up to us whether we'll be frightened enough to keep believing their promises will save us," Tom replied. A sudden jingle of the office door opening interrupted the conversation.

"Rebecca?" Emily asked, surprised to see her. "I thought you didn't work here anymore?"

"I don't," Rebecca replied. "Mary helped me find a fun new job at the comic store, and I love it there! Mike and I are taking her out to lunch."

"I knew it!" Mr Tuttle said with great relief. "That's so great to hear."

"I was scared and hoped politicians could save my job." Rebecca admitted. "But your dad was right— sometimes we just have to discover the best way forward... and I guess comics and games was mine!"

With another jingle of the door, Mike came in. "Hi, heroes!" he said. "I brought you something."

Mike presented the twins with replicas of the Ogre's helmet and the Sword of Truth.

"Demagogues don't stand a chance against this much truth!" Emily shouted, swinging it in the air.

"And your letter in the newspaper was spot on," Mike added. "So I brought you another book to learn more about the Leviathan in the real world."

"The truth will set us free... just be careful where you point the sword!" Rebecca chuckled.

"Ready to go, mom?" Mike asked, holding out his arm to Mary. "I think we should try out the new restaurant across the parking lot."

"Wait, Mary is your mom?!" the twins asked, almost in unison.

"Who do you think suggested I hire Rebecca at the store?" he smiled. "And now you know who *really* came up with all the ideas for our Team of Heroes quest..."

"So that's why the game was just like real life!" Emily said.

The End

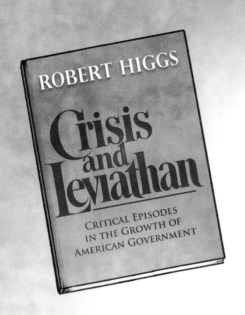

"The beginning of political wisdom is the realization that despite everything you've always been taught, the government is not really on your side; indeed, it is out to get you."

—Robert Higgs

Robert Higgs is an economist and scholar, and formerly a Senior Fellow at the Independent Institute. He has received numerous awards recognizing the impact of his writings.

Dr. Higgs is the author of many books, including *Crisis and Leviathan*, which analyzes U.S. history to demonstrate how government has repeatedly grown during times of crisis, without shrinking to its previous size and power after the crisis.

This book makes for compelling reading in an effort to understand the many changes made in the U.S. over the past century.